CW00551402

WHAT WOULD
DAVE GROHL
DO?

UPLIFTING ADVICE FROM THE
NICEST GUY IN ROCK & ROLL

POP PRESS

Pop Press, an imprint of Ebury Publishing
20 Vauxhall Bridge Road
London SW1V 2SA

Pop Press is part of the Penguin Random House group of companies
whose addresses can be found at global.penguinrandomhouse.com

First published by Pop Press in 2024

Design: Ed Pickford
Text: Liz Marvin
Illustrations: Ollie Mann

www.penguin.co.uk

A CIP catalogue record for this book is available from the British Library

ISBN: 9781529933307

Typeset in 10/14pt ITC Franklin Gothic LT Pro by Jouve (UK), Milton Keynes
Printed and bound in Great Britain by TJ Books Ltd, Padstow, Cornwall

The authorised representative in the EEA is Penguin Random House
Ireland, Morrison Chambers, 32 Nassau Street, Dublin D02 YH68

Penguin Random House is committed to a
sustainable future for our business, our readers
and our planet. This book is made from Forest
Stewardship Council® certified paper.

CONTENTS

INTRODUCTION

HOW TO LIVE LIKE DAVE GROHL

Dave Grohl is an insanely talented drummer, guitar player and songwriter. Yet he's also known as 'the nicest guy in rock', a devoted dad and a huge music fan. He's inspired generations while still seeming to be the kind of guy you could go for a beer with.

While not all of us are about to strap on a guitar and stride out on stage in front of thousands, there's a lot we can learn from this legendary frontman.

SHARE YOUR PASSION

Dave has said that when he first discovered punk rock in the early 1980s it changed his life. From then on, all he wanted to be was a musician. He believes passionately in music's power to connect people. He loves all genres of music and when he finds something he's into, he's never afraid to shout about it from the rooftops – or scream about it from the stage.

HAVE HEROES

No matter how famous he's become, Dave's never stopped being awed by his musical heroes, even though he's had the opportunity to play with most of them. From Paul McCartney to Robert Plant to Prince and many others besides. However, Dave's biggest hero is his mum, Virginia. Although she was a teacher at his school, she supported him when he wanted to drop out and go on the road with his band.

WORK HARD

While Dave has said he sometimes can't believe that what he gets to do every day is an actual job, there's no denying he's one of the hardest-working people in rock 'n' roll. He's collaborated with loads of different musicians, directed videos, written a bestselling book . . . Even when he fell off the stage and broke his leg, he refused to let the fans down, instead commissioning a custom-built throne he could perform from for the rest of the tour.

BUT PLAY HARD TOO!

Dave has always known that you can give something your all without having to be serious all the time. He once pranked an entire stadium into thinking he'd fallen off the stage again when he returned to the arena where he'd had his famous accident. It was only when he appeared on stage that the crowd realised the guy who had just pitched face first into the pit was actually Dave's stunt double.

GET BACK UP AGAIN

In fact, getting back up when you've fallen (or been knocked) down could be Dave's best advice. He has spoken openly about how he struggled to know how to go on after the death of his friend Kurt Cobain, and more recently he suffered the sudden loss of his musical soul mate, Taylor Hawkins. On both occasions, Dave has said that it was music that saved him.

LOVE EVERY MINUTE

Ultimately, if there's one thing that Dave would most like us to know it's this: make the most of everything you can because you don't know when it's going to end. Don't worry about being cool, about failing, about looking stupid – that's a waste of time and energy. Grab life with both hands. Scream as loud as you can and give it everything you've got.

MUSIC

'Music is something real and beautiful and it is fucking sacred.'

'I've always put focus
and emphasis on
pattern, composition
and arrangement.'

'There is nothing like the
energy and atmosphere
of live music. It is the
most life-affirming
experience.'

*'I look at the strings
on a guitar like it's a
drum set.'*

*'There will always be
rock 'n' roll.'*

'You can sing a song to 85,000 people and they'll sing it back for 85,000 different reasons.'

'We wouldn't go play shows that meant nothing to us. Every time we played it was blood and guts.'

'*My place in [Nirvana]*
was just to make as
much thunder as
I possibly could.'

'*Music is why I'm here. And all of the other craziness, when it becomes too overwhelming, I just retreat back into those sort of safe places.*'

' "Gangnam Style" is one of my favourite songs! What's wrong with that?!'

'With drums, I don't really have to think about it. It's like dancing. You don't have to think about dancing.'

[On performing]
'It doesn't matter how
bruised you get, doesn't
matter how thrashed
your voice is, or how
hungover you are, it feels
great every time.'

'If music's not enough,
not its own reward,
don't do it.'

'Making music is everybody's right.'

CREATIVITY

'The most important
thing is that whatever
you're doing, it's a
representation of
your voice.'

'If you have a natural
inclination and a real
drive to do something,
you can figure it out.
I really believe it's
that simple.'

'What you think, you become; what you feel, you attract; what you imagine, you create.'

'All you need are songs that deserve to be heard, a couple of friends and a genuine direction that you won't stray from.'

'Rock'n'roll has a history of being offensive. I think you have to be true to the person that you are, and it's inevitable that anything you say could go against someone else's feelings.'

'I'd rather see a band who looked like they were having a great time than just an evening out with their therapist.'

'Screaming bloody murder and playing as many notes as you can, that's fun. But to me, the complicated puzzle of braiding those things together in a way that seems simple is the greatest challenge.'

'I think once you start analysing anything you do too much you start to change and things aren't as pure as they were before.'

'There are choruses on this record that 50–fucking–thousand people are gonna sing, and it's gonna bring everyone's fucking hearts together in that moment.'

'It's YOUR VOICE.
Cherish it. Respect it.
Nurture it. Challenge it.
Stretch it and scream
until it's fucking gone
because . . . who knows
how long it will last.'

FAMILY

'My mother is my hero, she's a soldier, she's Joan of Arc, and I'm just some schmuck with a guitar, screaming at people.'

'When Kurt died
I realised that the most
important thing is life
and family and love
and happiness.'

'When you have kids, you see life through different eyes.'

'The whole dad rock thing? If you're lucky, you can stick around long enough that your own kid can be in your band.'

'Perhaps I love so fiercely as a father because mine could not.'

'My kids inspire me and it's that love that then when I go on the road, it makes me want to play music even more.'

'Kids can trash a dressing room faster than Van Halen. It's fucking insane.'

'My father was my first, and best, reader. It was through him that I found my love of writing.'

FRIENDS

'I'm one of those people
that just wants to share
everything with
everybody, whether it's
pain or joy, a song
or a drink.'

'It's important to me
that Foos stay best
friends and have the
camaraderie
of a great band.'

'Nirvana has become something other than a band of three people, but to me that's what it will always be, three individuals who made a few records and unfortunately stopped making records.'

'The reason we've been a band so long is we enjoy each other's company. There's not a lot of brooding and torture going on.'

'When I see a hero of mine, I run up and attack them with so much love.'

'If there's one thing I'm good at, it's gathering people together to do something fun.'

'When I was young, I didn't have sports or astronaut heroes. I had people who were friends of the family.'

[On Taylor Hawkins]
'The first time we had a beer together, we were like, we're gonna be best friends for life.'

GROWING UP

'I thought, "Maybe there's a world of weirdo like me out there," and it was just a matter of trying to find them.'

'There's a golden window
of opportunity in every
child's life where
independence and
identity intersect and
you're allowed to become
who you're going
to become.'

'I was the worst student in the school that my mother was a teacher at.'

'I learned to play guitar with a Beatles songbook and a Beatles record.'

'I had to get out and do something now or else sit on my ass forever.'

[On telling his parents that he wanted to drop out of school to be a musician] 'My mother was like "you better be good!"'

FAME

'I still have dreams that we're in Nirvana, that we're still a band. I still dream there's an empty arena waiting for us to play.'

'*The most difficult part is singing. And getting over the feeling that I look so stupid.*'

'I don't consider myself a frontman at all. Out of the four of us, I'm probably the least charismatic of everyone.'

'I'm not allergic to fashion. I'm just one of those people who when they put on a suit look like they're going to a funeral or to court.'

'I think if we're being honest women find me kind of, I don't know, funny looking.'

'I love being the guy headlining rock festivals with grey hair and wrinkles.'

[On being a rock star]
'I go out and scream for
three hours and then go
have pizza and beer.'

'It's funny; recently I've started to notice people's impersonations of me, and it's basically like a hyperactive child.'

'I wouldn't be able to do this if I didn't have my feet planted firmly on the ground.'

'I'm not the only nice guy in the history of rock'n'roll . . . I can be a fucking asshole too.'

'*I'm not the best drummer, I'm not the best guitar player, I'm not the best singer – but when I do any of those things, I do it like it's my first day on Earth.*'

COURAGE

'Courage is a defining factor in the life of any artist.'

*[On starting
Foo Fighters]*
'It was so incredibly
refreshing to go out and
do something where
you're frightened, really
scared to do it.'

'Don't waste a big moment on fear. Enjoy it, because it's never going to happen again.'

'I'm not the type of guy to go sky diving or bungee jumping, but I don't mind strolling out in front of 90,000 people and singing a song about love.'

[On making the first Foo Fighters album]
'I hated the sound of my voice and I questioned everything: my guitar playing, my songwriting, and especially my drumming. To strip it all bare was a real test.'

'Just knowing you've done something yourself makes you feel all the more satisfied.'

'You pick yourself up off
the ground. You walk
home. The show
must go on.'

*'One of the biggest
lessons is to know when
to say no.'*

'Life is just too damn short to let someone else's opinion steer the wheel.'

'I'm not afraid to write anything any more.'

SUCCESS

'I don't think I ever considered that conventional route.'

'If you're passionate, driven and focused in what you do, if you're really good at it, people will take notice.'

'I've never been a person who just retreats and stays in a comfortable place. I've always been one to move on.'

'Before I had any fucking money, I didn't care about money. Once I got money, I didn't care about money.'

'*I'm the type of person that says, "OK, let's figure this out," if I'm presented with a problem.*'

'You wouldn't imagine that going on tour keeps you in shape, but it actually does.'

'We just have to prove things to ourselves.'

'You be real, be true and be passionate and you have to honour the craft of making music. Everything else you just have to take with a grain of salt.'

'Throughout life, I've just tried to appreciate the things that maybe others can't.'

'*When we follow our hearts it ends up being really good.*'

'The key is to do something fulfilling, for which you get respect.'

'I'm the luckiest bastard
in the world.'

PHILOSOPHY

'The most important thing is that you be yourself.'

'In 1994 I had some sort of personal awakening or revelation or epiphany that life is worth living every single day.'

'*I realized no matter how good or bad a day,
I wanted to be alive to experience it.*'

'I don't believe in guilty pleasure, I just believe in pleasure.'

'*I'd never want to be a spokesperson for anything in case I said the wrong thing.*'

'*Guilt is cancer. Guilt will confine you, torture you, destroy you as an artist.*'

'You've got one life and you'd better live it as much as you can.'

'I believe in humility.'

'Fun has always been the priority for me, along with things that help me move forward as a person and as a musician.'

'Never tried heroin. Pills are lame. I like wine. I'm the fun drunk.'

'I found a lot of beautiful moments in things calming down.'

'I love what I do.'

'Sometimes, if you think about the good things that happened and take comfort in them, it sort of eases the pain of the bad.'

[On songwriting]
'I think one of the reasons why I'm so optimistic and hopeful and have the energy that I do is because I have somewhere to put vulnerability, insecurity, the darkest corners, rather than just bottle them up.'

'Everything that's happened up until now was just a happy accident. One day the happy accident will be that it ends.'

ACKNOWLEDGEMENTS

Epigraph from Off Camera with Sam Jones, 'Dave Grohl's Advice to Aspiring Musicians' (2013). P10 from Kerrang, 'I'm Still Standing' (1999). P11 from Edge Magazine, 'Dave Grohl: Reaching Drumming Nirvana (2011). P12 from The Atlantic, 'The Day The Live Concert Returns' (2020). P13 from NPR, 'Dave Grohl retraces his life-affirming path from Nirvana to Foo Fighters' (2021). P14 from Billboard, 'Dave Grohl Q&A: Why Rock Will Never Die & Why 2011 Was His Best Year Ever' (2012). P15 from The Guardian, 'Twenty years after In Utero, Nirvana's Importance hasn't diminished' (2013). P16 from The Guardian,' Dave Grohl: 'I never imagined myself to be Freddie Mercury" (2019). P17 from Music Week, 'The Aftershow: Dave Grohl' (2021). P18 from Dave Grohl, 'Storyteller' (2021). P19 from SXSW Keynote speech (2013). P20 from Apple Music, 'Dave Grohl: It's Electric! Interview (2017). P21 from Kerrang, "Touring the UK? It Feels Great Every Time!" (2005). P22 from Mojo, "everyone has their dark side" (2005). P23 from The Guardian, 'Dave Grohl: 'I never imagined myself to be Freddie Mercury" (2019). P26 from SXSW Keynote speech (2013). P27 from Napa Valley Film Festival, 'Sound City Q+A' (2013). P28 from Dave Grohl, 'Storyteller' (2021). P29 from from Kerrang, 'I'm Still Standing' (1999). P30 from The Standard, 'Dave Grohl: 'Musicians are human – their lives aren't yours' (2022). P31 from Melody Maker, 'Have We Got Foos For You!' (1995). P32 from Guitar World, 'Midnight Madness' (2021). P33 from NME, 'The Foo Epidemic' (1995). P34 from Kerrang, 'Dave Grohl On The New Foo Fighters Album: "It's Unlike Anything We've Ever Done"' (2020). P35 from SXSW Keynote speech (2013). P38 from Kerrang, '"Was This How I planned it? Not at all."'(2020). P39 from Kerrang, 'Big Mouth Strikes Again' (2002). P40 from TIME Magazine, 10 Questions (2009). P41 from Sunday Telegraph, 'Fighting On' (2021). P42 from The Sunday Times Magazine, 'Dave Grohl's Work/Life Balance' (2021). P43 from The Today Show (2021). P44 from Tinnitist.com, 'My 2011 Interview with Dave Grohl' (2011). P45 from The Atlantic, 'How Far Does the Apple Fall From the Tree? (2020). P48 from BBC News, 'Dave Grohl: My whole life is like an out-of-body experience' (2021). P49 from Man About Town, 'The LA Issue: Dave Grohl' (2011). P50 from The Ticket, 'The Chosen Foo' (2003). P51 from The Sunday Times, 'A Life in the Day: Dave Grohl' (2017). P52 from Waitrose Weekend, 'All My Life' (2021). P53 from Billboard, 'Dave Grohl on 'Sound City,' More Players Shows and Keeping McCartney Secret' (2013). P54 from Vox, 'Happy Dave is Here Again' (1997). P55 from Radio X, 'Dve Grohl in his own words' (2023). P58 from Channel 4 News, 'Dave Grohl on Nirvana's success, his musical awakening and stories from the road' (2021). P59 from The New Yorker Radio Hour, 'Dave Grohl's Tales of Life and Music' (2021). P60 from NPR, 'Dave Grohl retraces his life-affirming path from Nirvana to Foo Fighters' (2021). P61 from New York Post, 'Rocker Horror Picture Show' (2022). P62 from Melody Maker, 'The Chosen Foo' (1995). P63 from The Graham Norton Show (2021). P66 from Classic Rock, 'Let's Dance' (2021). P67 from Time Out, 'The Tao of Foo' (1995). P68 from Rolling Stone, 'It's a band, damn it.' (1995). P69 from GQ, 'GQ&A:Dave Grohl on Barry Manilow, Metallica and reuniting with Nirvana (2013). P70 from NME, '"I'm A Geek. I'm the Guy Next Door. Alright, Alright! I'm The Luckiest Bastard In The World!"' (2005). P71 from Man About Town, 'The LA Issue: Dave Grohl' (2011). P72 from The Late, Late Show with James Corden (2022). P73 from Spin, 'Q&A Dave Grohl' (2005). P74 from The Guardian, ''I've never gotten off on chaos" (2007). P75 from Metal Hammer, 'Mr Incredible' (2003). P76 from Financial

ACKNOWLEDGEMENTS

Times, 'Foo Fighters' Dave Grohl: 'I want to become a really wicked tap dancer" (2021). P80 from Dave Grohl, 'Storyteller' (2021). P81 from Blender, 'They Came from Outer Space' (1995). P82 from The Sunday Times, 'A Life in the Day: Dave Grohl' (2017). P83 from Live Magazine, 'Monster of Rock' (2007). P84 from Modern Drummer, 'Returning to His Roots With Probot' (2004). P85 from Melody Maker, 'What's The Frequency . . . Dave? (1999). P86 from Dave Grohl, 'Storyteller' (2021). P87 from NPR, 'Dave Grohl retraces his life-affirming path from Nirvana to Foo Fighters' (2021). P88 from Dave Grohl, 'Storyteller' (2021). P89 from The Guardian, "I've never gotten off on chaos'' (2007). P92 from The Independent, 'Dave Grohl on his childhood, career, and never wanting to live with an animal ever again' (2021). P93 from Napa Valley Film Festival, 'Sound City Q+A' (2013). P94 from Sunday Times Culture, 'Dave Grohl on Conflict Fame and Foo Fighters' New Album' (2021). P95 from The Guardian, 'Dave Grohl: 'You don't need a needle hanging out of your arm to be a rock star" (2014). P96 from OK!, 'Rock On!' (2021). P97 from Financial Times, 'Foo Fighters' Dave Grohl: 'I want to become a really wicked tap dancer" (2021). P98 from Kerrang, 'I'm Still Standing' (1999). P99 from The Tonight Show Starring Jimmy Fallon (2021). P100 from wbur.com, 'Dave Grohl explains how music — and a hitchhiker wearing a Kurt Cobain t-shirt — helped him heal' (2021). P101 from Kerrang, 'Dave Grohl On The New Foo Fighters Album: "It's Unlike Anything We've Ever Done"' (2020). P102 from Red Bulletin, '"You Just Grit Your Teeth and Get On With It"' (2017). P103 from NME, '"I'm A Geek. I'm the Guy Next Door. Alright, Alright! I'm The Luckiest Bastard In The World!"' (2005). P106 from BBC, 'The First Time with Dave Grohl' (2015). P107 from Classic Rock, 'Let's Dance' (2021). P108 from Vulture, 'In Conversation: Dave Grohl' (2021). P109 from Sunday Times Culture, 'Dave Grohl on Conflict Fame and Foo Fighters' New Album' (2021). P110 from Raw, 'Nirvana was Hilarious' (1995).

WHAT WOULD DAVE GROHL DO?

P111 from SXSW Keynote speech (2013). P112 from Q, 'Wheeeeeeeeeeeeeeeeeeee!' (1996). P113 from Man About Town, 'The LA Issue: Dave Grohl' (2011). P114 from Red Bulletin, ' "You Just Grit Your Teeth and Get On With It"' (2017). P115 from Rolling Stone, 'The Passion of Dave Grohl' (2014). P116 from NME, 'Dave Grohl tells us about Foo Fighters' 'Medicine at Midnight': "This is our Saturday night party album"' (2020). P117 from The Guardian, 'Dave Grohl: You don't need a needle hanging out of your arm to be a rock star" (2014). P118 from BBC News, 'Dave Grohl: My whole life is like an out-of-body experience' (2021). P119 from The Daily Telegraph, 'Glastonbury will be back – a pandemic can't kill it' (2021). P120 from Bang, 'On the Road with Foo Fighters' (2003).